HOW TO HAVE A
GOOD
LIFE

30 Daily Devotions from the
Sermon on the Mount

DANNY ZELAYA

Published by Danny Zelaya
DannyZelaya.com

Cover and Interior Design by Inspire Books
www.inspire-books.com

ISBN (paperback): 979-8-9869816-3-5
ISBN (hardback): 979-8-9869876-4-2
ISBN (ebook): 979-8-9869816-5-9

Library of Congress: 2024906866

Printed in the United States

*To my wife and four kids: May you
know God throughout your lives and
be used by him to bless others.*

How to Read this Book

This devotional is meant to be read over a thirty-day period at any time during the year. Each chapter can easily be read in the morning before work, during lunch, while parked in the car, or before going to bed. However, there are also different ways to use this devotional. Here are some suggested ways:

- **Read during seasons of growth.** There are times during the year when you may want to achieve spiritual growth, such as during the beginning of a New Year, the season of Lent and Easter, the summer reading period, the end-of-year holidays, or at any time where you want to dedicate thirty days of spiritual growth.
- **Personal study.** Use the two indices in the back of the book to guide your personal study. One index is thematic and shows you the key themes Jesus talks about. The second index is more detailed and focuses on the different topics covered in the devotional.
- **Group study.** Use the devotional as a group Bible study topic on the Sermon on the Mount. Spend thirty days as a group reading the devotional and supporting Scripture, and once a week

during Bible study, discuss any spiritual insights you've learned. This can foster a sense of community and shared growth.

- **Sermon preparation.** Pastors and leaders can use the key themes in the Key Themes Index for sermon topics or utilize the Detailed Topics Index to research supporting ideas and illustrations for their sermon preparations. This can help them connect the teachings of Jesus to contemporary life and make their sermons more relatable.

- **Reflections and prayers.** As you read each daily devotional, write down any thoughts, things to improve, or prayers to God in the notes section at the end of each chapter. Include the date of your writing. When you return to that devotional chapter in the future, you'll notice any growth you've achieved. Continue to write down a new date when writing a new entry. This practice can help you track your spiritual journey and see how God has been working in your life.

- **Read for inspiration.** You can read any chapter and the supporting Scripture as often as you'd like to remind yourself of the key ideas and uplifting message. Spiritual growth is always about coming back to the source of growth to sustain your motivation and focus. Don't hesitate to revisit the devotionals and supporting Scripture whenever you need a spiritual boost or guidance.

This devotional is simply a tool to help you grow closer to God and apply Jesus' teachings to your daily life. Choose the approach that works best for you, and be open to the Holy Spirit's guidance as you embark on this journey of spiritual growth.

Introduction

I wrote this devotional for the everyday person longing to live a good life filled with God's blessings. It's also written for those who can't attend church for various reasons. God's blessings are just as much for them.

The goal of this book is to introduce Jesus' Sermon on the Mount in a relatable, refreshed, and modern way. Jesus' teachings should speak straight to your heart in a simple way. Often, the truths of the Sermon on the Mount are underrepresented in sermons, theological writings, and creeds (formal statements of belief). Yet it is within these teachings that we discover God's presence in the ordinary moments of our lives. Indeed, it's in the everyday moments of our lives when we need divine guidance the most.

Jesus' sermon reveals that God is with us at home and at work just as much as at church. God is with us in the quiet, lonely moments just as much as when we raise our voices in song. He hears our hearts even when words elude us. Jesus assures us that our daily struggles and challenges will be a distant memory compared to the joy of living with God in the kingdom of heaven. Our lives have purpose, meaning, and direction.

In the Sermon on the Mount, we learn how to live according

to God's wishes and how to receive God's daily blessings. We learn how to live in harmony with others, in communion with God, and at peace with ourselves. The Sermon on the Mount is the blueprint for living a good life.

1

DAY

Blessed are the poor in spirit, for theirs
is the kingdom of heaven.

—Matthew 5:3

On the hillside, when Jesus begins teaching, his first lesson is on the attention God gives to those overlooked and undervalued by the world. He says good things belong to us when we don't have many good things going for us. God cares for us when we're feeling down, helpless, or in need.

Being *poor in spirit* can be understood in two different ways. First, it means you're self-aware of your limitations and rely on God's daily guidance, strength, and blessings. You acknowledge your limitations and your need for God's help. You seek and make room for God because you know and acknowledge your shortcomings. You're poor in spirit and rely on God's Spirit for strength, guidance, and direction.

Second, being poor in spirit means you have no spirit left in you. You feel helpless. The burdens of life weigh you down, and your enthusiasm for life is depleted. You may feel defeated by the harmful words and actions of others or by life's unpredictable trials.

When you're poor in spirit, God notices, and you're richly blessed and cherished by His Spirit. A divine, peaceful happiness is given to you. There's a confidence that uplifts your spirit.

The poor in spirit are loved, helped, and acknowledged by God. God's blessings belong to you, and good things await you. Joy and laughter will return to your spirit. When Jesus says, "Theirs is the kingdom of heaven," He is referring to the beauty of the heavens (the universe) and God's presence (spiritual) belonging to you. Beauty, wonder, hope, and strength are given to you. It is God's presence, strength, and guidance that give you the renewed confidence and enthusiasm to be rich in the spirit.

**God's richest blessings are reserved
for the humble and the helpless.**

DAY 1 REFLECTIONS

Blessed are the poor in spirit, for theirs
is the kingdom of heaven.

—Matthew 5:3

_____
_____
_____
_____
_____
_____
_____
_____
_____
_____
_____
_____
_____
_____
_____
_____
_____
_____
_____
_____

**God's richest blessings are reserved
for the humble and the helpless.**

2

Blessed are those who mourn, for they will be comforted.

—Matthew 5:4

A difficult reality of life is that things change. Nothing ever stays the same. Things begin, and things end. When things end, new things also begin. Nothing is as it once was. We will all experience the loss of something important to us. We can lose the job we had our hearts set on. Breakups in relationships happen. Friendships can disappear. Natural disasters, disease, evil acts, unfortunate accidents, and the normal passage of time cause us to lose our parents, children, family members, friends, and pets. Happiness and mourning are with us like the sun and the moon. There's morning and mourning throughout our lives.

We mourn the loss of what is dear to us. We also grieve when seeing the suffering of others. In the midst of our grief, fatigue, and heavy hearts, we can feel alone, confused, and without strength. Yet in our sadness, Jesus promises God's divine comfort. When you're sad or grieving, God offers you his divine comfort. The Greek word used for comfort (*parakaleó*) means God seeks you during your moments of grief. When you're comforted by God, he reaches toward you to bring you alongside him. He brings you next to him to encourage and strengthen you. He calls you by name to his side.

You're never alone or without comfort during your moments or seasons of grief. God is near to the brokenhearted and weary. You may be tired or have lost something important and dear to you, but when blessed by God, you always gain divine comfort and solace. You are always on God's mind, and God is always near you.

**In times of sadness, God draws you near
to give you comfort and strength.**

DAY 2 NOTES

Blessed are those who mourn, for they will be comforted.

—Matthew 5:4

_____

_____

_____

_____

_____

_____

_____

_____

_____

_____

_____

_____

_____

_____

_____

_____

_____

_____

_____

In times of sadness, God draws you near
to give you comfort and strength.

3

DAY

Blessed are the meek, for they will inherit the earth.

—Matthew 5:5

We often hear that to get ahead in this world, you must be aggressive and seek your place in history. We hear common phrases like, "All that matters is winning," "If you're not first, you're last," or "Claim your destiny." In the world of professional sports, the team that doesn't win the championship and places second can feel and believe they haven't accomplished anything despite their great achievements. We can believe that climbing the corporate ladder or achieving fame is what gives us meaning and a sense of accomplishment. We can also believe that displaying toughness and symbols of success are what earn us respect and self-worth. In this world, strength, money, and social status are highly valued.

People with power are celebrated and feared. Many seek after powerful positions that give social status, decision-making power, and wealth, and they are willing to lose what's most valuable to them to achieve it. It may, therefore, seem surprising that Jesus says those who are meek receive God's blessings. To be meek is to be gentle, kind, and patient. They don't retaliate or assert their power over others; they avoid conflict, and they are humble in heart.

Meekness does not mean weakness or passivity. Meekness is strength of character. You *choose* not to be forceful or argumentative. You choose to be kind and not easily offended, and when others try to challenge you, you respond with patience and kindness. There's a quiet confidence in being meek that brings with it peacefulness. Jesus describes *himself* as being meek and gentle (Matthew 11:29), and he encourages you to have the same character trait.

Society often applauds power and assertiveness. How does God honor and reward you for being meek? You inherit such wonders as the earth. You receive God's full blessings in this world and in the world to come. The last will be first and reign supreme with God. In a world that rewards aggression and power, your reward for being the opposite is a higher prize very few can achieve.

Keep your eyes on the prize.

God rewards you when you're humble, gentle, and kind. You will reign with God in the world to come.

DAY 3 REFLECTIONS

Blessed are the meek, for they will inherit the earth.

—Matthew 5:5

_____

_____

_____

_____

_____

_____

_____

_____

_____

_____

_____

_____

_____

_____

_____

_____

_____

_____

God rewards you when you're humble,
gentle, and kind. You will reign with
God in the world to come.

4

DAY

Blessed are those who hunger and thirst for
righteousness, for they will be filled.

—**Matthew 5:6**

We desire good things in our lives. We enjoy the sun's warmth on our skin, sharing laughter with friends, eating savory food, listening to inspiring music, traveling to new destinations, reading books that stimulate our minds, cherishing love, spending quality time with family, celebrating achievements, and enjoying the simple pleasures of life. We desire a life of contentment, peace, and fulfillment.

But things don't always turn out as we want them to. Life's unpredictability can reveal its unfair side. Misfortune, inequality, and random events can overshadow the happiness in our lives.

We have a deep desire for a world with justice, fairness, and goodness. Jesus recognizes and affirms our desire. Even when we're tired and disillusioned from the unfairness of life, Jesus assures us that our desire for righteousness is not in vain. He says we're blessed to have this desire for good and righteousness. We find favor in God's eyes.

Jesus promises that your desire for righteousness and justice will be fulfilled. Your persistence will be rewarded. This assurance should inspire you to lead a righteous life and see righteousness prevail in the world.

When you're hungry and eating at a good restaurant, the food you eat creates a memorable experience. The feeling of pleasure and satisfaction from eating delicious food is similar to the happiness your soul will experience when your desire for righteousness is fulfilled by God. You'll be pleased and satisfied with God's justice and righteousness.

**Embrace your desire for righteousness.
Keep working toward it daily, confident
that it will be satisfied by God.**

DAY 4 REFLECTIONS

Blessed are those who hunger and thirst for
righteousness, for they will be filled.

—Matthew 5:6

_____

_____

_____

_____

_____

_____

_____

_____

_____

_____

_____

_____

_____

_____

_____

_____

_____

_____

_____

**Embrace your desire for righteousness.
Keep working toward it daily, confident
that it will be satisfied by God..**

5

DAY

Blessed are the merciful, for they will be shown mercy.

—Matthew 5:7

When I was a teenager, I played baseball in a low-income area of Los Angeles. The field was old and brown, with holes in the ground. Across town, a new league opened up in a nicer area. The field was beautiful and green. I wanted to play in this new league, but I couldn't afford the high cost.

I gathered enough courage to ask the coach if they needed an assistant to help gather balls, move equipment, or keep track of statistics. I figured that way, I could at least learn from the players and practice with them. The coach knew I played Little League and asked why I wasn't joining the newer league in town. I told him I couldn't afford the fee. Learning about where I lived and my circumstances, he offered me a significant discount to join the team. I was elated and thrilled at his kindness and quickly joined the team. Newly motivated, I was always the first to arrive early at every practice. I wasn't as good as the other players, but the coach gave me a chance to join the team and play.

Being merciful means expressing kindness and compassion toward others. Yet it goes beyond sympathy for others. To be merciful is to actually *do* something about a person's challenging situation. You help alleviate their suffering and improve their circumstances. Mercy is a divine action toward others. It's a reflection of divine grace in motion.

When mercy is shown to others, many blessings occur. First, there's divine reciprocity toward us. As we show mercy, God shows us mercy. Furthermore, we are blessed by God. God looks favorably upon us and blesses us (*blessed are the merciful*). Acts of mercy also draw us closer to God's divine nature. We mirror God's nature when merciful toward others. And through our compassion, we help others in need and transform their lives, much like how that coach changed mine.

Showing mercy brings you closer to God. You are blessed by God and grow closer to his likeness.

Day 5 Reflections

Blessed are the merciful, for they will be shown mercy.

—Matthew 5:7

_____
_____
_____
_____
_____
_____
_____
_____
_____
_____
_____
_____
_____
_____
_____
_____
_____
_____
_____
_____
_____
_____

❧

Showing mercy brings you closer to God. You are blessed by God and grow closer to his likeness.

6

DAY

Blessed are the pure in heart, for they will see God.

—Matthew 5:8

There are many things we do to experience God. We memorize Scripture, attend church services, participate in Bible studies, listen to Christian music, or adhere to specific diets. Some people travel the world to spiritual locations to encounter God's presence, while others remain local and in solitude. We can believe that we have to do great things, be perfect, or follow strict religious rules to see God. But Jesus says none of these things are needed. We do not need to do great things or be perfect to see God. All we need is a sincere heart that is devoted to him.

Pure in heart also means clean in heart. You have a clear heart without corrupt desires, thoughts, or motivations. You keep yourself clean from thoughts, desires, or actions that can corrupt you. A pure heart is a genuine and sincere heart with integrity. It is free from evil. There are no ulterior motives, and it's transparent for everyone to see. Having a pure heart does not mean you're perfect or can't make mistakes. It means you strive to live an upright life without any hypocrisy.

What's your reward for having a pure heart? Jesus says you will see God. Just as clear water reflects the sun, a pure heart reflects God's presence in your life. You receive a special and divine relationship with him. What Jesus says in this verse can also be translated as "for they God will see."[1] God sees you as well.

You can be of humble means and feel unimportant, but God notices you and continues to be with you. Great charisma or great acts are not needed to see God. A pure, sincere, and clean heart devoted to God is all that's needed. The pure in heart are happy and blessed, and they will inherit eternal life. They see God in this life and in the life to come.

When we have a pure heart, we are blessed with a special relationship with God.

---

[1] *Bible Hub Interlinear Bible*, https://biblehub.com/interlinear/.

DAY 6 REFLECTIONS

Blessed are the pure in heart, for they will see God.

—Matthew 5:8

When we have a pure heart, we are blessed
with a special relationship with God.

7

DAY

Blessed are the peacemakers, for they
will be called children of God.

—Matthew 5:9

I look like my dad, and as I get older, the resemblance gets closer. But my calm disposition, easy-going way, and sweet tooth are from my mom. Do you resemble your mom and dad? You tend to have similarities with your parents. When you look like them, you hear phrases like, "You have your mom's eyes," or "You have your dad's smile." Similarly, if a child looks like you, they might be called your "mini-me."

We can also behave like our parents, and our children can behave like us. When people say phrases like, "The apple doesn't fall far from the tree," or "Like father, like son," they mean a person behaves or has similar character traits as their parent.

How do we recognize God's children? One defining characteristic that distinguishes the followers of Jesus is their pursuit of peace. Jesus says the true children of God are peacemakers.

Peacemakers reflect God's nature of harmony and reconciliation. It's not enough to just believe in peace or recite it in a creed. Peacemakers actively *create* peace between people and between people and God. They desire and work for peace. They bring people together and remove any discord that causes conflict and separation. They create peace rather than conflict or division. The goal of all relationships is friendship. By reflecting God's nature, peacemakers bring people together to create greater unity in others and within themselves. Peacemakers help God bring reconciliation to the world.

True peacemakers must first cultivate peace within themselves. It's impossible to promote peace within others and yet be a divisive person. We cannot promote peace and yet raise our voices at others; we cannot create unity and yet exclude others; we cannot believe in peace and yet say or do things that create conflict within others.

A peacemaker actively seeks to promote peace and reconciliation. A troublemaker, on the other hand, fuels conflict and division.

God blesses you when you're a peaceful person and create peace between people.

DAY 7 REFLECTIONS

Blessed are the peacemakers, for they
will be called children of God.

—Matthew 5:9

_____

_____

_____

_____

_____

_____

_____

_____

_____

_____

_____

_____

_____

_____

_____

_____

_____

_____

_____

_____

_____

**God blesses you when you're a peaceful
person and create peace between people.**

8

DAY

Blessed are those who are persecuted because of righteousness, for theirs is the kingdom of heaven.

—Matthew 5:10

Doing what's right is difficult when it may lead to rejection or opposition. There are times when we do the right thing, and our reward is to be mistreated by others. This can happen in many situations:

- At work, you report a leader's misconduct and receive retaliation like group exclusion or a stalled promotion.
- At church, you express concern over a leader exploiting people, and you're removed from serving in the church or bullied in response.
- In your family, you maintain different values and convictions, and you're judged or excluded from family events for being different.
- In politics, you vote according to your conscience, but it's not what your political party approves. You are criticized by your own party as a result.

- In your country, you stand up for what is right and are jailed.

Jesus acknowledges that living a righteous life can be challenging. Living out your values isn't easy when it leads to being mistreated and criticized. Yet Jesus affirms that persevering in doing the right things leads you to being blessed by God. The reward for a life of integrity is a home in God's kingdom. It's a place where those who have suffered mistreatment for being faithful to God's values are vindicated and honored by God.

If you're criticized and persecuted for living God's values, remember that you're blessed by God. He gives you the divine strength and peace to persevere. You're also in good company with the prophets and apostles who've walked your path. When you're driven away (the literal meaning of "persecuted") by others, you are driven into God's presence. God welcomes you into the kingdom.

**God divinely blesses you for living a life
of integrity and doing what's right.**

DAY 8 REFLECTIONS

Blessed are those who are persecuted because of
righteousness, for theirs is the kingdom of heaven.

—Matthew 5:10

God divinely blesses you for living a life
of integrity and doing what's right.

9

DAY

You are the salt of the earth. But if the salt loses its
saltiness, how can it be made salty again? It is no longer
good for anything, except to be thrown out and trampled
underfoot. You are the light of the world. A town built on
a hill cannot be hidden. Neither do people light a lamp
and put it under a bowl. Instead they put it on its stand,
and it gives light to everyone in the house. In the same
way, let your light shine before others, that they may
see your good deeds and glorify your Father in heaven.

—Matthew 5:13–16

It's normal to feel inadequate sometimes and believe others possess greater talents. Yet God has given us all distinctive talents and abilities, waiting to be uncovered and embraced. Our life's journey is to identify and use them to bless others. Our task is to have faith in God as he guides us to discover them. We must trust God's process of revelation.

Jesus describes us as the salt of the earth and light of the world. As salt, we are to preserve and enhance the good in this world. We're to do good and create optimism in a world filled with pessimism and conflict. Salt retains its good qualities *unless* it is contaminated. Similarly, we can diminish our potential by neglecting our talents or making poor decisions in life. This is the meaning of salt losing its saltiness and of salt becoming tasteless. If we withhold doing good, our gifts aren't revealed, and we don't make the world a better place.

Jesus also describes us as the light of the world. We are to remove darkness with our inner brightness. We shine a light by following God's kingdom values, being a positive influence, and bringing out the best in others. By following God's Word and embodying Jesus' teachings, we reflect God's divine light, and people see God through us.

God's light brings life all around us. Darkness grows in this world when we allow it to grow. When we remain silent to wrongdoing, allow lies to persist, and make little effort to reflect God's values, darkness steadily grows. Quiet consent allows darkness to take root.

You must stand firm as a visible lighthouse. Illuminate the path through darkness and be a source of faith, love, and hope. You are the salt of the earth that preserves good and the light of the world that guides to the truth.

You are the best of the earth. Live out your faith to make a positive impact on the world and on those around you.

DAY 9 REFLECTIONS

In the same way, let your light shine before
others, that they may see your good deeds
and glorify your Father in heaven.

—Matthew 5:16

You are the best of the earth. Live out
your faith to make a positive impact on
the world and on those around you.

10

DAY

Therefore anyone who sets aside one of the least of
these commands and teaches others accordingly
will be called least in the kingdom of heaven, but
whoever practices and teaches these commands will
be called great in the kingdom of heaven. For I tell
you that unless your righteousness surpasses that
of the Pharisees and the teachers of the law, you
will certainly not enter the kingdom of heaven.

—Matthew 5:19

In Jesus' day, he encountered religious leaders who appeared righteous on the surface. Their righteousness was based on following religious routines and rituals, but they ignored the more important requirements of love, mercy, forgiveness, and humility. The religious leaders followed the religious routines, but in their hearts and minds, they weren't aligned with God's heart. By forcing their rules on others, they made life difficult for others while making life easier for themselves.

In every church, there are rules, customs, and traditions that we are expected to follow. These traditions are what support the culture. But we can mistakenly believe that following religious routines is the same as having a personal relationship with God. It is not. Religious routines keep us disciplined in growing in love and mercy, but if we miss the compassion behind the routines, our hearts are not spiritually transformed.

You don't enter the kingdom of heaven by how closely you follow church rules and customs. You enter the kingdom of heaven by allowing God to change your heart and mind. It's about having your heart aligned with God's heart. Focus on the transformation of your heart and mind that leads to a life of love, grace, mercy, forgiveness, and humility. Following rules may grant you acceptance into a group but won't grant you access into the kingdom. A life of faith that is aligned with God's values and that comes from the sincerity and obedience of your heart is what grants you access into the kingdom.

God doesn't want group conformity but rather a genuine relationship with him that changes your heart and mind.

DAY 10 REFLECTIONS

Whoever practices and teaches these commands
will be called great in the kingdom of heaven.

—Matthew 5:19

God doesn't want group conformity but rather a genuine relationship with him that changes your heart and mind.

11

DAY

You have heard that it was said to the people long ago,
"You shall not murder, and anyone who murders will
be subject to judgment." But I tell you that anyone
who is angry with a brother or sister will be subject to
judgment. Again, anyone who says to a brother or sister,
"Raca," is answerable to the court. And anyone who says,
"You fool!" will be in danger of the fire of hell. Therefore,
if you are offering your gift at the altar and there
remember that your brother or sister has something
against you, leave your gift there in front of the altar.
First go and be reconciled to them; then come and offer
your gift. Settle matters quickly with your adversary who
is taking you to court. Do it while you are still together
on the way, or your adversary may hand you over to the
judge, and the judge may hand you over to the officer,
and you may be thrown into prison. Truly I tell you,
you will not get out until you have paid the last penny.

—Matthew 5:21–26

Anger is a normal human emotion. It's a common reaction
to situations where we feel treated unfairly, powerless, or
hurt or when our beliefs are challenged. But harboring and
nurturing anger is unhealthy and harmful to us. Anger can cloud

41

and close our minds with hateful thoughts and resentment. When angry, we ignore the good things and people in our lives.

Anger can lead to violence if it is not managed in a healthy way. Anger is what causes people to insult ("Raca!" "You fool!"), hate, and harm others. Jesus says that murder *and* anger are both judged by God ("subject to judgment") because internalized anger leads to hateful thoughts, feelings, and acts toward others and ourselves. Uncontrolled anger corrodes the love, compassion, and beauty we are created to reflect.

If you have internalized anger and resentment toward yourself or others, you must resolve your anger in a positive way. This means actively working to not harbor negative thoughts and feelings and seeking reconciliation. Prayer and attending church can be helpful tools for building and healing relationships, but they are not the only things needed. Jesus tells us to *reconcile* with anyone we're angry with or who has anger against us. Resolving conflicts is more important than religious offerings or religious piety. Living peaceably with others is an essential part of our faith.

If you have anger toward someone, address and resolve your anger; and if someone is angry at you, attempt to make things right with them.

Being a Christian involves the challenging task of seeking peace even in difficult circumstances. In a family, parents want all their kids to love, get along with, and support one another. In God's family, God wants the same for his children.

Make peace with everyone, including yourself.

Day 11 Reflections

Therefore, if you are offering your gift at the
altar and there remember that your brother
or sister has something against you, leave
your gift there in front of the altar.

—Matthew 5:23–24

Make peace with everyone, including yourself.

12

DAY

You have heard that it was said, "You shall not commit adultery." But I tell you that anyone who looks at a woman lustfully has already committed adultery with her in his heart. If your right eye causes you to stumble, gouge it out and throw it away. It is better for you to lose one part of your body than for your whole body to be thrown into hell. And if your right hand causes you to stumble, cut it off and throw it away. It is better for you to lose one part of your body than for your whole body to go into hell.

—Matthew 5:27–30

Today, Jesus talks to us about the importance of guarding our thoughts and desires. We often think of sin as the physical actions we take, but Jesus teaches us that sin actually begins in our thoughts and desires. Sin begins in our hearts and minds, and our thoughts, desires, and intentions can be just as wrong as committing a wrongful act.

In discussing adultery, Jesus says clinging to lustful thoughts or lustful desires for someone other than your spouse is wrong. Affairs begin in the mind and heart. They often occur with someone you know, such as a longtime friend, a friend of your spouse, a coworker, or someone you interact with frequently. The familiarity with the person makes it easier for an affair to begin, but the formed emotional attachment makes it hard to end. Affairs lead to devastating pain for the people involved, as well as to their children, family, and friends.

Love and lust are different. Lust is a desire to acquire someone (or something) to fulfill your emotional or sexual needs. It appreciates only what you can get from them, while love appreciates a person for who they are. Love desires to give, whereas lust is only interested in receiving.

To protect your thoughts and desires, be vigilant about what you allow yourself to think and do. Be mindful of the repeated situations that lead you to have lustful thoughts and desires. Avoid the triggers that cause you to have such thoughts and feelings, and pay attention to how you interact with others, particularly on social media.

Instead of nurturing lustful thoughts and desires, focus on nurturing the thoughts, desires, and actions that lead to love and faithfulness.

Guard your thoughts and desires by paying attention to what you think and do.

DAY 12 REFLECTIONS

If your right eye causes you to stumble, gouge it out and throw it away. It is better for you to lose one part of your body than for your whole body to be thrown into hell.

—Matthew 5:29

Guard your thoughts and desires by paying
attention to what you think and do.

13

DAY

It has been said, "Anyone who divorces his wife must give her a certificate of divorce." But I tell you that anyone who divorces his wife, except for sexual immorality, makes her the victim of adultery, and anyone who marries a divorced woman commits adultery.

—Matthew 5:31–32

Today, Jesus addresses the significance of commitment in marriage. Marriage is a voluntary commitment we enter into, but once formed, it's a holy bond. It's a commitment to love one another despite the highs and lows of life. We commit to working through issues together, compromising, sacrificing when needed, and prioritizing the union over selfish pursuits. We choose a *shared* life in a marriage.

The word Jesus uses for divorce means to release and dismiss someone. In his time, divorce was often used by men to dismiss their wives for arbitrary reasons. This created economic and social hardship for women when they were divorced. Jesus limits the justifiable reasons for divorce to infidelity. It's important to note that Jesus doesn't list all the valid reasons for divorce since that's not his intention. His focus is on the commitment of a marriage. It's not something to enter into lightly or end quickly.

Marriage has its challenges, and it can be tempting to want to leave your spouse when you are experiencing disagreement or dissatisfaction in your relationship. It might also be tempting to consider leaving for someone else who seems more understanding, exciting, or compatible. But these thoughts and emotions are fleeting, and your commitment to your spouse is based on love, which is enduring, resilient, patient, and forgiving.

In a world where relationships are easily formed and dissolved, Jesus calls us to uphold a higher standard of commitment, faithfulness, and love within a marriage. Marriage is a lifelong journey of growth, companionship, and deepening love. Marriage is a reflection of God's love.

You have a higher standard of commitment, faithfulness, and love within a marriage.

DAY 13 REFLECTIONS

But I tell you that anyone who divorces his wife, except
for sexual immorality, makes her the victim of adultery.

—Matthew 5:32

_____

_____

_____

_____

_____

_____

_____

_____

_____

_____

_____

_____

_____

_____

_____

_____

_____

_____

_____

❧

You have a higher standard of commitment,
faithfulness, and love within a marriage.

❧

14

DAY

Again, you have heard that it was said to the people long ago, "Do not break your oath, but fulfill to the Lord the vows you have made." But I tell you, do not swear an oath at all: either by heaven, for it is God's throne; or by the earth, for it is his footstool; or by Jerusalem, for it is the city of the Great King. And do not swear by your head, for you cannot make even one hair white or black. All you need to say is simply "Yes" or "No"; anything beyond this comes from the evil one.

—Matthew 5:33-37

Oaths and promises are common in many areas of life and serve as a pledge to do something, but they are not actually needed to do what you say.

Jesus tells us not to make oaths because overpromising leads to negative consequences. If a person makes an oath to God to never lie and then lies, they break that oath and may feel guilt or shame. By making oaths, we are claiming more than we should. We claim more power to fulfill them than we actually possess.

Oaths can lead us to make claims that we can't fulfill, and they're often made for show. People make oaths to impress others and to show seriousness. But public declarations are not needed to do what we say. In fact, they can be misleading because we give a false impression of our true intentions and capabilities.

In making oaths, we are promising control over something that is beyond our power. We can't guarantee we will never make a mistake, and we can't change the color of our hair no matter how hard we try. We lack control over many aspects of our lives. When we make oaths we can't keep, we disappoint ourselves and others. We can lose credibility as people start to doubt our trustworthiness.

Instead of making oaths, Jesus tells us to just be honest and trustworthy. Let that alone be the foundation of our words and actions.

Simply be trustworthy and honest.

DAY 14 REFLECTIONS

Do not swear by your head, for you cannot
make even one hair white or black. All you
need to say is simply "Yes" or "No."

—Matthew 5:36–37

_____

_____

_____

_____

_____

_____

_____

_____

_____

_____

_____

_____

_____

_____

_____

_____

_____

_____

_____

_____

Simply be trustworthy and honest.

15

DAY

You have heard that it was said, "Eye for eye, and tooth
for tooth." But I tell you, do not resist an evil person.
If anyone slaps you on the right cheek, turn to them
the other cheek also. And if anyone wants to sue you
and take your shirt, hand over your coat as well. If
anyone forces you to go one mile, go with them two
miles. Give to the one who asks you, and do not turn
away from the one who wants to borrow from you.

—**Matthew 5:38–42**

We often hear people say things like, "Fight back,"
"Stand your ground," and "Get even." These phrases
encourage us to retaliate against a perceived enemy.
In Jesus' day, the popular phrase was, "Eye for eye, and tooth for
tooth." This meant it was acceptable to retaliate against someone as
long as it was proportional to the wrongdoing.

Retaliation is the act of responding to harm or wrongdoing with
another form of harm. Retaliation is praised because it's seen as a
sign of strength and a way to get even with someone. We retaliate
because we don't want to be thought of as weak by others. Society
looks favorably on retaliation, but Jesus says retaliation is not the
path of Christians. He is against retaliation. When Jesus says not to

resist an evil person, he means not to repay a wrong with a wrong. We refuse to do evil by retaliating.

Instead of responding with a wrong, you respond with a right. By turning the other cheek (refusing to do evil), you respond with a kingdom action. You respond to evil with grace, kindness, and generosity—these are kingdom values. You weaken the aggressor's power to create conflict by responding with kindness. You maintain your integrity and peace, and this prevents you from descending into anger and spite.

If someone insults you, and you respond with kindness, they may be surprised and ashamed of their behavior. Their misconduct is transparent to them (and others), and this can lead to a change of heart. Although no abuse should ever be tolerated, by responding to an injustice with grace, you respond with a different power and truly change the outcome. You respond with the power and values of the kingdom.

Don't retaliate when someone offends you, but respond with grace, kindness, and generosity.

DAY 15 REFLECTIONS

If anyone forces you to go one mile, go with them two miles. Give to the one who asks you, and do not turn away from the one who wants to borrow from you.

—Matthew 5:41–42

Don't retaliate when someone offends you, but
respond with grace, kindness, and generosity.

16

DAY

You have heard that it was said, "Love your neighbor and hate your enemy." But I tell you, love your enemies and pray for those who persecute you, that you may be children of your Father in heaven. He causes his sun to rise on the evil and the good, and sends rain on the righteous and the unrighteous. If you love those who love you, what reward will you get? Are not even the tax collectors doing that? And if you greet only your own people, what are you doing more than others? Do not even pagans do that? Be perfect, therefore, as your heavenly Father is perfect.

—Matthew 5:43-48

It's normal to like supporters and dislike critics or those who challenge us. Loving our enemies is difficult because they have wronged us or represent views we disagree with. Political parties, for example, thrive on criticizing other political parties. We show favoritism to people with similar views and hostility toward those with opposing views. We like the people in our group ("*love your neighbor*") and dislike the people outside it ("*hate your enemy*"). But Jesus teaches us to do something different. Jesus teaches us to live an extraordinary life by being kind to our enemies and praying for their well-being.

To love our enemies means to want the best for them, even when they have wronged us. It means to pray for them and treat them with kindness. It doesn't mean we agree with their views or their behavior. But it does mean that we choose to respond to them with kindness rather than hate. Instead of wanting bad things to happen to them, we want the opposite. We wish good things for them just as we would wish good things for ourselves.

Loving your enemies requires removing hateful feelings toward them, and this begins with changing your beliefs and views about them. You decide your attitude toward them, regardless of how they feel about you. When you pray for your enemies, you seek a change in them but also within yourself. You ask God to change *your* heart and mind.

Prayer helps us become extraordinary people. Through prayer, we transition from resentment to forgiveness and from hatred to compassion. In loving the people we dislike and wishing good things for them, we grow into what Jesus describes as "perfect." To be perfect is to be spiritually whole, complete, and mature.

You grow in spiritual perfection by reflecting God's compassion and good deeds to everyone. This is what it truly means to be children of God and followers of Christ.

**Be kind and compassionate to the people
who challenge you, and change your beliefs
through prayer. Be perfect and extraordinary.**

DAY 16 REFLECTIONS

You have heard that it was said, "Love your neighbor and hate your enemy." But I tell you, love your enemies and pray for those who persecute you, that you may be children of your Father in heaven.

—Matthew 5:43–45

Be kind and compassionate to the people
who challenge you, and change your beliefs
through prayer. Be perfect and extraordinary.

17

DAY

Be careful not to do good deeds in front of other
people. Don't do those deeds to be seen by others. If
you do, your Father in heaven will not reward you.
When you give to needy people, do not announce it
by having trumpets blown. Do not be like those who
only pretend to be holy. They announce what they
do in the synagogues and on the streets. They want
to be honored by other people. What I'm about to
tell you is true. They have received their complete
reward. When you give to needy people, don't let your
left hand know what your right hand is doing. Then
your giving will be done secretly. Your Father will
reward you, because he sees what you do secretly.

—Matthew 6:1–4, NIRV

In today's digital world, it is easy to be influenced by social
media and the desire to be seen and praised by others. This can
lead us to do things for attention, including doing good deeds.
We can do good deeds to be seen by others because we want praise
and recognition. But Jesus warns us not to do good deeds just for
attention.

When you do a good deed and then publicize it to receive

recognition, or when you do good because you know you'll get attention, your motives are not pure. You want people to see and praise you for what you've done. You're motivated by the admiration of people rather than the obedience to God's will.

Jesus tells us to do good deeds without fanfare. Genuine good deeds are motivated by a love for God and a compassionate desire to help others. They are done without the expectation of praise or reward. Our motives can become quickly contaminated by seeking people's approval and praise. When we do good deeds in secret, our motives are pure and rooted in a compassionate desire to help others.

Do good deeds in a normal way with a heart that doesn't seek recognition or praise from others (*don't let your left hand know what your right hand is doing*). God knows your heart and sees what you do in secret and openly rewards you with blessings.

Do good deeds with a pure heart without seeking attention and recognition. God will reward you.

DAY 17 REFLECTIONS

Be careful not to do good deeds in front of other
people. Don't do those deeds to be seen by others. If
you do, your Father in heaven will not reward you.

—Matthew 6:1

Do good deeds with a pure heart without seeking
attention and recognition. God will reward you.

18

DAY

When you pray, do not be like those who only pretend to be holy. They love to stand and pray in the synagogues and on the street corners. They want to be seen by other people. What I'm about to tell you is true. They have received their complete reward. When you pray, go into your room. Close the door and pray to your Father, who can't be seen. Your Father will reward you, because he sees what you do secretly. When you pray, do not keep talking on and on. That is what ungodly people do. They think they will be heard because they talk a lot. Do not be like them. Your Father knows what you need even before you ask him. This is how you should pray.

"Our Father in heaven, may your name be honored. May your kingdom come. May what you want to happen be done on earth as it is done in heaven. And forgive us our sins, just as we also have forgiven those who sin against us. Keep us from sinning when we are tempted. Save us from the evil one."

Forgive other people when they sin against you. If you do, your Father who is in heaven will also forgive you. But if you do not forgive the sins of other people, your Father will not forgive your sins.

—Matthew 6:5–15, NIRV

We talk to God and build a relationship with him through prayer. It's a simple act, but it can sometimes feel difficult to know how to do it right. There are so many different ways to pray, and it can be hard to know which way is best. People kneel, bow their heads, raise their hands and voices, and perform ceremonial acts. When observing the different ways to pray, it can seem difficult to know if God is listening.

Jesus simplifies what we have made so complicated. Jesus tells us to pray privately and sincerely with him. Talk to him as you would a friend. What matters is the honesty and openness of our hearts.

What should you pray about? Anything and everything. God already knows your needs and circumstances, so there's no need for fancy or rehearsed phrases. Just talk and be open. Be yourself. Share your struggles, questions, and needs. Ask for guidance when making decisions and ask for strength to forgive and get along with others. If you have no words, God hears your thoughts and feelings. No words are better than memorized words that go through the motions.

God cares more about the openness of our hearts than the quantity of our words. The most important thing is to be honest with him. We don't need to use fancy words or phrases. We just need to be ourselves and talk to God from our hearts.

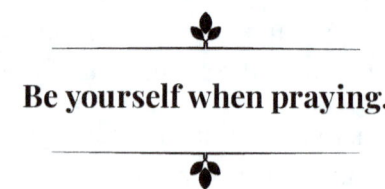

Be yourself when praying.

DAY 18 REFLECTIONS

When you pray, go into your room. Close the door and
pray to your Father, who can't be seen. Your Father will
reward you, because he sees what you do secretly.

—Matthew 6:6

_____
_____
_____
_____
_____
_____
_____
_____
_____
_____
_____
_____
_____
_____
_____
_____
_____
_____
_____
_____

❧

Be yourself when praying.

19

DAY

When you fast, do not look somber as the hypocrites
do, for they disfigure their faces to show others
they are fasting. Truly I tell you, they have received
their reward in full. But when you fast, put oil on
your head and wash your face, so that it will not be
obvious to others that you are fasting, but only to
your Father, who is unseen; and your Father, who
sees what is done in secret, will reward you.

—Matthew 6:16–18

Jesus warns us against performing spiritual practices just to get
the attention and admiration of others. He gives us the example
of fasting, but it can be any religious act, such as preaching,
praying, praising, or baptizing others.

When we perform spiritual practices just to get people's attention, we are hypocrites. We are putting on a pious show for others, but our hearts are not in the right place. We are not really interested in devotion to God. Instead, we are only interested in getting praise, likes, and recognition from people. An outward show of religion can hide an inward absence of true devotion to God.

When fasting or doing any spiritual practice, do it discreetly without showmanship. Don't broadcast what you're doing to everyone. Like washing your face as a daily routine, when practicing your faith, appear as you normally do every day. Aim inward toward God, and not outward for praise and attention.

Practicing our faith daily yet discreetly, we are showing God that our motives are pure. When fasting, for example, we temporarily give up food to focus on our reliance and dependence upon God. This gives us greater awareness of our human fragility and helps us appreciate the good things we have that we take for granted. And when we fast with a sincere heart, God rewards us.

Act normal when fasting or practicing your faith. God sees and rewards your sincerity.

DAY 19 REFLECTIONS

When you fast, put oil on your head and wash your
face, so that it will not be obvious to others that you are
fasting, but only to your Father, who is unseen; and your
Father, who sees what is done in secret, will reward you.

—Matthew 6:17–18

_____ ❧ _____

**Act normal when fasting or practicing your
faith. God sees and rewards your sincerity.**

_____ ❧ _____

20

DAY

Don't store up treasures here on earth, where moths
eat them and rust destroys them, and where thieves
break in and steal. Store your treasures in heaven,
where moths and rust cannot destroy, and thieves
do not break in and steal. Wherever your treasure
is, there the desires of your heart will also be.

—Matthew 6:19–21 NLT

One truth about life is that change is constant and inevitable. Our jobs evolve, friendships change, and children grow up. Even our views and beliefs tend to shift over time. Becoming too attached to things that change or don't last can lead to disappointment. A life centered around clinging to the past, pursuing money, or seeking external validation results in stress, worry, and unfulfillment.

Change is inevitable, but there are things on earth that hold enduring worth because they continue for eternity. These are the things that Jesus says are "treasures in heaven." Such things as love, kindness, forgiveness, and mercy carry eternal worth. Kingdom values are treasures that last forever. They reflect God's heart, and they bring you happiness, peace, and fulfillment. Jesus encourages you to focus on acquiring these kingdom values instead of being so focused on things of earthly value that fade, such as the pursuit of money, possessions, social status, and power.

By prioritizing kingdom values, the things that come and go in this world are put into perspective. You may still experience disappointment, but with a heart focused on acquiring kingdom values, you'll have comfort, peace, and assurance, knowing your spiritual investments have eternal worth.

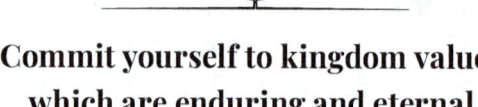

Commit yourself to kingdom values, which are enduring and eternal.

Day 20 Reflections

Wherever your treasure is, there the
desires of your heart will also be.

—Matthew 6:21

_____

_____

_____

_____

_____

_____

_____

_____

_____

_____

_____

_____

_____

_____

_____

_____

_____

_____

_____

**Commit yourself to kingdom values,
which are enduring and eternal.**

21

DAY

Your eye is like a lamp that provides light for your body.
When your eye is healthy, your whole body is filled with
light. But when your eye is unhealthy, your whole body
is filled with darkness. And if the light you think you
have is actually darkness, how deep that darkness is!

—Matthew 6:22–23 NLT

I n baseball, it's common to hear a coach tell their batters they have a "good eye." When a batter is facing an opposing pitcher and the batter does not swing at a bad pitch that's near the strike zone, they are said to have a good eye. These players have an excellent awareness of the strike zone and can quickly judge what pitches to swing at and which to avoid. As a result, they frequently get on base to help the team score. A batter that has a "bad eye" constantly swings at bad pitches and strikes out.

When we have a good eye, we have good judgment, and good judgment is essential for making wise decisions in life. When we have a bad eye, we make poor choices.

Jesus describes our eyes as lamps that give light to our lives. Where we direct our eyes influences our thoughts, desires, and actions. If our eyes are good, we have pure motives and make good choices. There's no dishonesty or deceit, and our character shines. But when our eyes are bad, our motives, decisions, and actions are bad. We're led by selfish desires. Just as a batter with a bad eye is more prone to errors, directing our focus toward unwholesome things can lead us astray, causing us to miss out on God's true blessings.

What you focus on influences your direction in life. If you have a good eye rooted in kingdom values, you don't swing at the bad pitches of life. You have good judgment, motives, and spiritual insight into reality. If you follow God's will, your life will be illuminated. But if you're led by bad and selfish desires, you will constantly strike out at life.

Focus on good and upright things, and you'll avoid swinging at the bad pitches of life.

DAY 21 REFLECTIONS

Your eye is like a lamp that provides light
for your body. When your eye is healthy,
your whole body is filled with light.

—Matthew 6:22

Focus on good and upright things, and you'll
avoid swinging at the bad pitches of life.

22

DAY

No one can serve two masters at the same time.
You will hate one of them and love the other. Or you
will be faithful to one and dislike the other. You
can't serve God and money at the same time.

—Matthew 6:24 NIRV

I n yesterday's reflection, Jesus emphasized the dangers of
self-deception. If you think you're righteous and can't acknowledge your flaws or bad habits, the righteousness you think
you have is actually darkness. You can't see or acknowledge your
shortcomings.

In today's teaching, Jesus talks about another form of
self-deception. He says you cannot be equally loyal to God and
money. One is more important to you and will have most of your
attention. The meaning of *mammon* is typically money, but it also
means jewelry, luxury items, and material possessions. Mammon
is the pursuit of riches, and it consumes your attention. The literal
translation says *you don't have the power or the ability* to serve two
masters, and yet many people try without noticing the consequences.
You will always prefer one over the other, and you may not realize it.

Jesus tells us that pursuing God and wealth are incompatible.

Pursuing large fortunes will take your attention away from God and other important areas of your life, such as your family, friends, and health. Self-deception happens when you falsely believe you're serving God (or your family), but in reality, you're pursuing fame, power, and money.

Money is your master when most of your time and attention is focused on getting rich. The pursuit of riches will distract you from your kingdom values and from spending time with God. Instead, prioritize a relationship with God by reassessing your use of time.

You can't be committed to God while devoted to money, fame, and power.

DAY 22 REFLECTIONS

You can't serve God and money at the same time.

—Matthew 6:24

You can't be committed to God while
devoted to money, fame, and power.

23

DAY

I tell you, do not worry. Don't worry about your life and what you will eat or drink. And don't worry about your body and what you will wear. Isn't there more to life than eating? Aren't there more important things for the body than clothes? Look at the birds of the air. They don't plant or gather crops. They don't put away crops in storerooms. But your Father who is in heaven feeds them. Aren't you worth much more than they are? Can you add even one hour to your life by worrying? And why do you worry about clothes? See how the wild flowers grow. They don't work or make clothing. But here is what I tell you. Not even Solomon in all his royal robes was dressed like one of these flowers. If that is how God dresses the wild grass, won't he dress you even better? Your faith is so small! After all, the grass is here only today. Tomorrow it is thrown into the fire. So don't worry. Don't say, "What will we eat?" Or, "What will we drink?" Or, "What will we wear?" People who are ungodly run after all those things. Your Father who is in heaven knows that you need them. But put God's kingdom first. Do what he wants you to do. Then all those things will also be given to you. So don't worry about tomorrow. Tomorrow will worry about itself. Each day has enough trouble of its own.

—Matthew 6:25-34 NIRV

Every morning, while it's still dark outside, the birds in the trees outside my house sing. One bird begins chirping, and soon other birds follow. They sing to start their day, and they sing because they're not worried. They don't worry about career ambitions, buying expensive things, or societal expectations. They sing every morning because their focus is always on today's blessings.

We worry when we're uncertain about things. Our constant worrying leads to stress, anxiety, and missing out on life's daily blessings. Worrying doesn't change a situation. It makes us inward-focused and blinds us to the wonders around us. We miss out on life's daily, beautiful moments when we're worried.

Jesus recognizes our tendency to worry and tells us not to worry so much. He tells us three times to "do not worry" in the passage. God is aware of what we need, and he will provide. By encouraging us to observe nature, Jesus reminds us of God's care. God designed the beautiful birds and flowers we see, and if God takes care of something so small as a flower, won't God do much more for us, who are made in his image?

Nature relies on God's care, and so should you. Observe the beauty of nature and remember God cares for you.

The birds remind us of the beauty of living today. Just as they trust nature's daily rhythm, we must daily trust in God's care and plan for us. By trusting in God to provide what we need, we open our eyes and hearts to receive God's blessings.

**Focus on today's blessings and trust
in God daily to provide what you need.
Don't forget to sing every morning.**

DAY 23 REFLECTIONS

Look at the birds of the air. They don't plant or gather
crops. They don't put away crops in storerooms.
But your Father who is in heaven feeds them.
Aren't you worth much more than they are?

—Matthew 6:26

Focus on today's blessings and trust
in God daily to provide what you need.
Don't forget to sing every morning.

24

DAY

Do not judge other people. Then you will not be judged.
You will be judged in the same way you judge others.
You will be measured in the same way you measure
others. You look at the bit of sawdust in your friend's
eye. But you pay no attention to the piece of wood in
your own eye. How can you say to your friend, "Let
me take the bit of sawdust out of your eye"? How can
you say this while there is a piece of wood in your own
eye? You pretender! First take the piece of wood out
of your own eye. Then you will be able to see clearly
to take the bit of sawdust out of your friend's eye.

—Matthew 7:1–5 NIRV

We tend to judge others while overlooking our own
shortcomings. Judging others makes us feel better
about ourselves. We judge others by what we say,
think, and do. We *say* things to put people down, *do* things like
exclude them from important events we invite others to, and *think*
negative thoughts about them.

When you judge, you make yourself the standard you measure
others by. You compare yourself to others, and by judging them, you
make yourself feel more important than them. Yet this does little to

change or improve your life. By judging others, you can lose out on making new friends, miss self-improvement opportunities, and you don't address the source of your own unhappiness.

Jesus' message to us is clear and straightforward: Don't judge anyone. It's a guideline for living a good life. By judging others, we ignore our own flaws, and this reveals us as hypocrites. Since no one is perfect and everyone has imperfections, we should always approach others with humility and compassion.

It's easier to make friends when you don't judge them. Instead of making enemies by judging others, make friends by understanding them. Avoiding judgment also makes it easier for you to not be bothered by the people who judge you. A nonjudgmental person does not pay attention to giving or receiving judgment.

Instead of being quick to judge others, focus on an attitude of gratitude and self-improvement. You can make more progress by practicing compassion over criticism and by improving yourself than by trying to mold others into your image by criticizing them. God loves the people you judge. They are made in the image of God. Don't tear down what God has built up.

Be mindful of your own shortcomings, and always approach others with compassion.

DAY 24 REFLECTIONS

First take the piece of wood out of your own
eye. Then you will be able to see clearly to take
the bit of sawdust out of your friend's eye.

—Matthew 7:5

_____

_____

_____

_____

_____

_____

_____

_____

_____

_____

_____

_____

_____

_____

_____

_____

_____

_____

_____

_____

_____

Be mindful of your own shortcomings, and always approach others with compassion.

25

DAY

Do not give holy things to dogs. Do not throw your
pearls to pigs. If you do, they might walk all over them.
They might turn around and tear you to pieces.

—Matthew 7:6 NIRV

Gratitude comes with understanding the value and meaning of something. Kids, in their innocence, often struggle to appreciate the true worth of things. They don't know the hard work that goes into earning money or the sentimental value something carries. When grandparents, even with limited means, offer a small gift of their love to their grandchildren, it's the emotional significance of the gift that truly matters.

We all have the desire to share our frustrations and joys with those around us. Sometimes, we want to vent, express disappointment, or share good news. Sharing gives us renewed strength, and it increases our trust in the person with whom we share. We like to share what's important and interesting with others. Prayer, for example, is a form of sharing between us and God.

Who you share with is also important. Some people are unable, unwilling, or untrustworthy to value or respect what's shared with them. They're at a place in life where they can't appreciate what you share with them. Sharing with them is counterproductive because they dismiss what you say and how you feel. Your precious "pearls" representing love, when given to the unappreciative, are underappreciated.

Jesus tells us to exercise good judgment when sharing something valuable with others. When sharing our pearls of wisdom and opening our hearts to share, we should do so with people who are receptive and trustworthy.

Remember also to appreciate when others share their pearls of wisdom. You may likewise fail to appreciate the importance of what's shared with you.

Be careful who you share your valuable pearls with, and be attentive when others share their valuable pearls with you.

DAY 25 REFLECTIONS

Do not throw your pearls to pigs. If you do,
they might walk all over them. They might
turn around and tear you to pieces.

—Matthew 7:6

_____

_____

_____

_____

_____

_____

_____

_____

_____

_____

_____

_____

_____

_____

_____

_____

_____

_____

_____

_____

_____

Be careful who you share your valuable
pearls with, and be attentive when others
share their valuable pearls with you.

26

DAY

Ask, and it will be given to you. Search, and you will find. Knock, and the door will be opened to you. Everyone who asks will receive. The one who searches will find. The door will be opened to the one who knocks. Suppose your son asks for bread. Which of you will give him a stone? Or suppose he asks for a fish. Which of you will give him a snake? Even though you are evil, you know how to give good gifts to your children. How much more will your Father who is in heaven give good gifts to those who ask him!

—Matthew 7:7–11 NIRV

Loving parents want the best for their children. When parents see something their child might love, they think of the joy their child will have by receiving it. If a child has a favorite meal their parent makes, the child receives enjoyment from eating it, and the parent receives joy from making it. Parents give good things to their children because they love them. A parent's happiness is often intertwined with their children's happiness. Both receive joy from the act of giving and receiving.

Loving parents give good gifts. Likewise, our heavenly Father, overflowing in love, wants to give even greater gifts to his children. The gifts God gives you align with your needs and his divine will.

Many of us wrestle with approaching God with our needs and desires. We can believe we aren't good enough or question whether God truly listens. But Jesus says that God is not hard to find. God is always accessible, eager to listen, and responds to all our requests. All we have to do is ask.

Does that seem too easy? Why do we believe it's hard? Have we been taught to believe asking *should* be hard? Whenever we knock through prayer, God welcomes us. Whenever we need guidance, strength, or purpose, all we need to do is ask God.

Challenge yourself to embrace this truth: Everyone who asks receives if it aligns with God's will. Try it. Try it daily this week and see if your life begins to change. Approach God with faith, sincerity, and persistence. Know that he cares for you and responds to you.

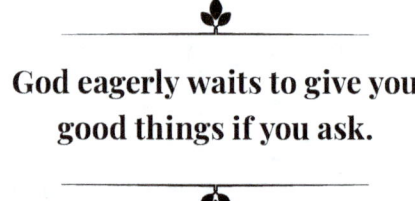

**God eagerly waits to give you
good things if you ask.**

Day 26 Reflections

Even though you are evil, you know how to give good
gifts to your children. How much more will your Father
who is in heaven give good gifts to those who ask him!

—Matthew 7:11

_____
_____
_____
_____
_____
_____
_____
_____
_____
_____
_____
_____
_____
_____
_____
_____
_____
_____
_____
_____
_____
_____

**God eagerly waits to give you
good things if you ask.**

27

DAY

Therefore in all things, whatever you want that
people should do to you, thus also you do to
them. For this is the law and the prophets.

—**Matthew 7:12 LEB**

There's a simple way to make new friends, do God's will, and
create a meaningful change in society. It doesn't require
you to become a politician, preacher, or influencer. You
don't have to be charismatic or a leader. What is this simple way?
Do to others what you would want them to do to you. If you want
to be treated in a certain way, act that way toward others. By doing
what's good, you teach others what is good to do. In this way, people
begin to change, and it starts with you taking the initiative to do
the good you desire and want to see. A ripple effect of change begins
with your actions.

All the good we hope for and all the kindness we seek originates
from God. God gives his best to us, and, in turn, we give our best
to others. We pass on the blessings we've been given.

There are other common ways to summarize what Jesus says:

- Be the leader you wish you had.

- Be the best person you wish you could become.
- Live up to how you want to be remembered.
- Embody the values you want your children to have.
- Mentor others at work in the way you wish you had been mentored.
- Lead others with the compassion and integrity you seek in leadership.
- Parent with the love and patience you wish you had received.
- Welcome others at church with the warmth and acceptance you desire.

The Golden Rule is a command from God in how to treat others, including those unkind to you. But it's also a guideline to follow if you desire to change society for the better. In all areas of life (*"in all things"*), the good you want to see is the good you should do. You teach others the right actions to follow. They observe and learn, and things begin to change. There's power in following the Golden Rule.

**How you want to be treated is
how you should treat others.**

DAY 27 REFLECTIONS

Therefore in all things, whatever you want that people should do to you, thus also you do to them.

—Matthew 7:12

_____
_____
_____
_____
_____
_____
_____
_____
_____
_____
_____
_____
_____
_____
_____
_____
_____
_____
_____
_____
_____
_____

**How you want to be treated is
how you should treat others.**

28

DAY

Enter God's kingdom through the narrow gate. The gate
is large and the road is wide that leads to ruin. Many
people go that way. But the gate is small and the road
is narrow that leads to life. Only a few people find it.

—Matthew 7:13–14 NIRV

During the summer, many people take road trips to national parks. For the people who've driven long distances, they wait patiently to get in. Once inside, joy and excitement replace any fatigue or frustration they may have experienced on the journey to their destination. The beauty of the moment makes the trip worth it.

Jesus talks about two contrasting roads that each lead to a destination. One path promises self-seeking pleasure. The path is alluring and shallow, and one simply follows the crowd. The path leads to a lack of purpose and fulfillment. Then, there's the narrow road rarely taken because it requires discipline and commitment to God's will. The path can be challenging but leads to meaning, purpose, and fulfillment. Genuine faith requires you to take this path.

On this narrow and disciplined path, you'll often make tough choices. You'll say *no* to the things that lead you away from this path, and you'll say *yes* to the core values that sustain your direction. This is the path to God's kingdom, and it's the right way of life that brings you peace and fulfillment, both in this life and the next.

There are few who choose this path, but it's the path that leads you to eternal life. The beauty of the destination makes the journey worth it.

Walk the narrow path of discipline and devotion to God's will. It's the path into his kingdom.

DAY 28 REFLECTIONS

But the gate is small and the road is narrow
that leads to life. Only a few people find it.

—Matthew 7:14

Walk the narrow path of discipline and devotion
to God's will. It's the path into his kingdom.

29
DAY

Watch out for false prophets. They come to you
pretending to be sheep. But on the inside they are
hungry wolves. You can tell each tree by its fruit.
Do people pick grapes from bushes? Do they pick
figs from thorns? In the same way, every good tree
bears good fruit. But a bad tree bears bad fruit. A
good tree can't bear bad fruit. And a bad tree can't
bear good fruit. You can tell each tree by its fruit.

—Matthew 7:15–20 NIRV

In every age, people have sought to protect what's dear to them.
Militaries use sophisticated radar and sonar systems to differentiate between friend and foe. Farmers use fences and pesticides
to protect their crops and livestock from potential harm. People
install cameras and alarm systems to protect their homes. In Jesus'
time, watchtowers were used to look out for friendly visitors, harmful
animals, or enemies.

Jesus urges the same kind of alertness. He warns us of those appearing righteous on the outside yet hiding harmful intents inside.
"Watch out for false prophets" means to be on the lookout *and* hold
your course. Don't let up. These people appear righteous, but their

true nature is driven by selfish motives, and they're willing to deceive to get what they want. They're always deceptive and destructive.

To help identify someone's true intentions, Jesus tells us to pay attention to their actions ("fruits"). A person's actions can reveal their true character. A good person, represented by a healthy tree, is someone who lives with integrity, generosity, and compassion. Their actions enrich others' lives. A bad person, represented by a diseased tree, is someone driven by selfish motives. They take from people rather than give and create conflict between them. Their diseased fruit corrupts people.

Jesus tells us to be watchful when people claim to represent God or use Scripture to proclaim their own ideas. A person's true character, motives, and personal beliefs are reflected through their actions.

Pay attention to what people do. Outward appearances can deceive, but actions rarely lie.

Day 29 Reflections

A good tree can't bear bad fruit. And a bad tree can't
bear good fruit. You can tell each tree by its fruit.

—Matthew 7:18–20

———————————————————————
———————————————————————
———————————————————————
———————————————————————
———————————————————————
———————————————————————
———————————————————————
———————————————————————
———————————————————————
———————————————————————
———————————————————————
———————————————————————
———————————————————————
———————————————————————
———————————————————————
———————————————————————
———————————————————————
———————————————————————
———————————————————————
———————————————————————
———————————————————————
———————————————————————

❧

Pay attention to what people do. Outward appearances can deceive, but actions rarely lie.

30

DAY

Not everyone who says to Me, "Lord, Lord," will
enter the kingdom of heaven, but the one who does
the will of My Father who is in heaven will enter.
Many will say to Me on that day, "Lord, Lord, did
we not prophesy in Your name, and in Your name
cast out demons, and in Your name perform many
miracles?" And then I will declare to them, "I never
knew you; leave Me, you who practice lawlessness."

—Matthew 7:21–23 NASB

Yesterday, Jesus told us to watch out for false leaders, teachers, and preachers who deceive by appearing honest but, in reality, are dishonest. Jesus tells us to pay attention to their actions for clues to who they really are. Today, he talks to us about those who feel their religious deeds secure eternal salvation.

Jesus warns that simply doing religious acts doesn't mean we truly know him. Religious deeds disconnected from a personal relationship with him are misguided efforts. Claiming to speak for God while our hearts are far away from him reveals a shallow faith. Listening to God and living by his teachings are what matter. God values our obedience over merely following church rules, professing beliefs, or going through the motions at church.

Surprisingly, the people who are famous for displaying their faith might actually be far from heaven. This is because showing off your faith doesn't guarantee entry into heaven. What really counts is leading a life that aligns with God's teachings, having sincere faith, and earnestly following God's will.

Many people quietly follow God's will, and even though they don't show off, God notices them clearly. God values the many who faithfully serve him, and those we least expect might be the closest to entering his kingdom.

It's not about who publicly affirms God. It's about those who genuinely obey and align their lives to his will that find a place in God's kingdom.

DAY 30 REFLECTIONS

Not everyone who says to Me, "Lord, Lord," will
enter the kingdom of heaven, but the one who does
the will of My Father who is in heaven will enter.

—Matthew 7:21

It's not about who publicly affirms God. It's about
those who genuinely obey and align their lives
to his will that find a place in God's kingdom.

Key Themes Index

This thematic index highlights the key themes and core messages of the Sermon on the Mount. It groups related topics together, making it easier for you to grasp the overarching lessons and principles of Jesus' teachings. This index is ideal for spiritual growth, study groups, and sermon topics.

Detailed Topics Index

This detailed index is perfect for in-depth personal study or research. It's designed to help you quickly locate specific topics, themes, and key concepts discussed in the Sermon on the Mount. This index is ideal for learning about a specific topic, seeking guidance on a particular issue or challenge, and finding relevant passages to support your lessons, discussions, or personal growth.

About the Author

Danny Zelaya serves as a chaplain in the California Army National Guard and as an Executive Director at a Fortune 500 company. He applies the lessons of faith to both his military and corporate leadership roles.

Danny is the author of the acclaimed book *Managing Your Habits for Success*, which is also featured on getAbstract.

He holds master's degrees in theological studies and philosophy from Claremont School of Theology and Claremont Graduate University.

To stay updated on Danny's weekly writings, you can find him on Facebook, Instagram, LinkedIn, and TikTok. For signed copies of his books, which include a personal note from the author, please visit www.dannyzelaya.com.